Train Up a Child

A story about my personal experience with alcoholism

"Train up a child in the way he should go. And when he is old, he will not depart from it"

- Proverbs 22:6 (KJV)

Keoshia Banks

Copyright @ 2019 Keoshia Banks

All rights reserved. No part of this book may be reproduced, stored in a retrieval system or transmitted in any form or by any means, electronic, mechanical, including photocopying, recording, or by any information storage or retrieval system, without permission in writing from the publisher.

Dedication

This book is dedicated to anyone who has struggled with breaking a generational curse that has been passed down to you.

I pray that God will continue to strengthen you daily as you take on this heavy burden. The good news is that God created you for this task and he will never put more on you than you can handle. He is your strength and through you, your family bloodline will be changed. Don't give up!

Acknowledgments

I would like to take time to thank God for giving me the desire and boldness to write this book. And for his grace and mercy. From the stories I tell in this book, you will see, I should have been dead. But even when I turned my back on God, he kept me! I'm so grateful that he protected me.

I would also like to thank my spiritual mom and dad, Pastor and Co-Pastor Simpson, for being committed to following God's call on their lives. Daniels Den Ministries is literally the place where God shut the lion's mouth. The lion in my life was known as alcoholism.

Last but certainly not least, I want to thank my mom. First for letting me put her in a vulnerable place so that I can tell my story and second for doing her best to raise me! We have experienced a lot together, and I love her so much.

I would further like to take the time to apologize to anyone I ever hurt due to poor word choice or bad decision making when I use to drink/get drunk. From the bottom of my heart, I am sorry!

Introduction

"Train up a child in the way he should go. And when he is old, he will not depart from it"

- Proverbs 22:6 (KJV)

Usually, when people quote this scripture, they are referring to raising children in the ways of the Lord with the expectation that when the child becomes an adult he or she will not turn away from God. The truth is this scripture can be applied to less favorable habits as well. For example, if you raise a child in ways of lying, cheating, drinking or stealing, when he grows older, he will not depart from those behaviors. That is unless that person encounters God's transforming power.

This is a story about how I was trained to be a functional alcoholic and how only the healing and delivering power of Christ was able to redirect my path.

Side Note: Please understand that due to the trauma I experienced as a child, my memory is distorted. Some of the experiences mentioned may have taken place one or two years before or after the actual age written. Despite this discrepancy, the experiences are real.

Chapter 1
Alcoholic In Training

"May I have a strawberry daiquiri with whipped cream and a strawberry on top," my mom ordered while we are out dining.

"Mom, can I have one too?" says eight-year-old me.

"Yes, Keoshia."

"Can I have a virgin strawberry daiquiri, with extra whipped cream and a strawberry on top please?" I asked the waitress.

My mom, stepdad, brother and I were out eating at one of our favorite restaurants, Ruby Tuesday. We ate there at least once a month. My mom enjoyed cooking but by the time Sunday came around she needed a break, so we made going out to eat after church a family tradition. Most of the time it was just me, my mom and my brother but this time my stepdad finally decided to go to church with us.

"Did you enjoy the service," I asked my stepdad.

"Yeah, it was pretty cool. I'm going to go next Sunday too."

I wasn't sure if he was telling the truth because he told a lot of fibs, but I really was hoping he would.

I did not know much about God yet, but I had a feeling that if my stepdad started going to church regularly, he would become a better man.

See my stepdad was a compulsive liar, a heavy drinker and I later learned he was also abusive.

He did not start out that way though.

When I first met him, he was really loving toward my mom and both me and my brother. He treated us like we were his own children. When my mom would work long hours, he would let me talk his ear off. He was really involved in our lives.

I remember one time I was heading to a birthday party and my hair was a hot mess. There was no way on earth I was leaving the house without getting my hair done.

My mom was a hairstylist, so my hair had to be done at all times.

My mom was really busy at work that day, so my stepdad offered to help me out. He was a barber, but I had no idea that he knew anything about doing hair. To my surprise, he put my hair in a neat ponytail, and I was all set for the party.

This was one of many acts of love my stepdad would display toward me. From cookies and milk snack breaks to trips to the hardware store where he'd push me through the store on the back of the cart. We truly had a lot of fun together.

That was until he got hurt on his job.

A few months after he hurt his back at work, I noticed a change. He started drinking more. He would leave the house and be gone all day. Sometimes I wouldn't even see him because he would come home after I was already in bed. His behavior led to years of hurt and pain, but I will save that for a different book.

We left the restaurant and headed home. Our stomachs were so full that all we could do was take naps when we got home.

The house was so calm and peaceful that I napped for two hours.

When I woke up, I helped my mom clean up the house. The house was always clean, so it didn't take long.

After I finished, it was time to get ready for bed, so I could wake up well rested for school the next day.

I was a student at Brookside Elementary in Grand Rapids, MI. One of the brightest in my class if you ask me.

No, really! I was a bright student and truly loved school. I liked all of my teachers and I had a lot of friends. On top of that, I always maintained good grades.

Being a stellar student as well as a cheerleader and dancer kept me out of trouble at home. In a way, I was able to slide through the cracks because my mom didn't feel like she had to worry about me much.

My school was about a 20-minute walk from our house, so my brother and I walked to and from school every day.

One day when we were walking home, my brother and I were talking and as usual, we started arguing. To this day, I have no idea what we were arguing about, but I took off running. Every time he would try to catch up to me, I would run even further ahead of him. He started crying but because we were arguing I thought it was funny.

Yes, I know. That was mean.

My brother and I were close in age but for some reason, we did not get along with each other while we were growing up. It might have been because we grew up around abuse and arguing or it could have been sibling rivalry. Whatever it was, sometimes we really went at it against each other.

When I got home, I waited at the door before going in, so it could seem like we arrived at the same time. As soon as we got into the house, he told on me.

"Mom, Keoshia left me when we were walking home from school," he told her.

"Keoshia, why did you leave your brother," asked my mom.

"I didn't." I replied.

She left it alone.

That was one of those times when being a good student got me out of trouble and possibly why my brother and I didn't get along. He was always getting in trouble and somehow, I was always getting away with stuff.

I went straight to my room, so I could avoid my brother until he calmed down.

Later that night we had one of our usual weekend parties.

There was never a special occasion for these parties, my mom just liked having people over on the weekends. She loved to cook so she cooked a bunch of food and invited friends and family over to play cards, listen to music and eat.

While the adults partied all night in the basement, us kids played video games and watched movies upstairs. Every now and then we would sneak downstairs acting like we were thirsty or hungry, so we could see what was going on.

When the adults were not paying attention, I use to sneak a few Jell-O shots out of the refrigerator.

They were so good!

It always seemed like the adults were having the time of their lives. Even over the loud music, I could hear them laughing.

Sometimes the parties did get out of hand though.

One time, one of my aunts had a drunken fit and started taking off her clothes in the living room. She was butt naked, screaming and yelling as if she was possessed by the devil. She even called the police on herself.

Other than the few times people would completely lose their minds, those parties were the best part of the week. I remember thinking "I can't wait until I am grown and can throw these same fun parties at my house every weekend."

This is where it all started. The weekly parties, virgin strawberry daquiris, and the tasty Jell-O shots started my journey to what I consider functional alcoholism.

Chapter 2
This Is What Being Drunk Is Like

After graduating from sixth grade, I went on to middle school. I attended two different middle schools, one for seventh grade and a different one for eighth.

Life at home had gotten pretty rough, so I tried to stay as busy as possible with dance, cheer, and school. I even tried basketball just to give myself something else to do.

During my middle school years, my stepdad's drinking problem had worsened. I can't remember a time when he wasn't drunk. One evening when I was warming up some food in the microwave, my mom and stepdad started arguing.

My mom had just gotten home from a long day of work.

She came in complaining as usual.

She was complaining to him about how one of his sons was being disrespectful to her.

My mom and stepdad were always arguing about something, but this time was much different than others. Maybe because my stepdad was really drunk.

I am not sure of the real reason, but I knew I needed to get out of the way.

I took off running up the stairs with my fork still in my hand. I stood at the top of the stairs waiting for them to finish their argument so that I could go back downstairs to get my food.

Bang!

I heard a loud sound come from the kitchen.

"Let me go, let me go!" my mom yelled. It sounded like she was running from the kitchen to the living room near the bottom of the stairs.

The yelling was followed by a series of loud punches. I could hear each blow loud and clear. My mom was screaming for her life and I was crying hysterically.

I ran to my brother's room, but he laid like a brick in his bed. I knew he was not sleep because who could sleep with all of the noise, but he would not move. I went into my mom and stepdad's room, grabbed the house phone and dialed 911.

I ran into my room and locked the door.

"911, what's your emergency?"

"Please help, my stepdad is beating my mom." I cried on the phone.

"Does he have a weapon?"

"I don't know. Just please send someone. Help!! Please!!"

"Okay, help is on the way."

I hung up the phone and sat in my room, praying to God with all of my heart. It felt like forever had gone by, but the police still hadn't gotten to the house.

I called back.

"Did you send someone yet?"

"Yes, someone is on their way."

"Keoshia, Keoshia open the door," my mom whispered gently.

I opened the door and sat on my bed. I was so scared I could have peed my pants. When she walked into the room her eye was the size of a golf ball and it was completely black. She sat down on the bed and hugged me tightly. My mom was so strong, she wasn't even crying. She consoled me until we heard police sirens outside.

I pulled back from her embrace, looked at her and without a word she smiled. She kissed me on the forehead and headed downstairs.

I tiptoed down the stairs to look out of the side window. I saw my stepdad being handcuffed and put inside the back of the police car. Despite what he had done to my mom, I was sad to see him being taken away. I was really going to miss having him around.

I didn't have to miss him very long though because it wasn't long before he returned.

One night my mom called my brother and me to the basement for a family meeting.

My stepdad was there.

My mom looked at me and my brother with both sorrow and joy in her eyes. I know that might be hard to imagine but that is the best way I can explain the look on her face.

My stepdad spent about 5 minutes pleading his case, telling us about how sorry he was and begging for our forgiveness.

As much as I loved and missed him while he was gone, I had no desire to forgive him. I was afraid of him and knew at this point the relationship we had would never be the same.

When he was finished talking, my mom asked if we would welcome him back into the house.

I was shocked.

More than anything in the world I wanted my mom to be happy. I looked at my brother to see what he would say.

My brother was a very quiet kid and barely reacted with much emotion, so he just shrugged his shoulders and looked at me.

I felt like I was stuck between a rock in a hard place. Here I am, a child, having to make what felt like the biggest decision in my life.

On one hand, I wanted him gone. I never wanted to experience the level of fear I felt the day he beat my mom. But on the other hand, I wanted my mom to be happy.

What do you think I did?

I welcomed him back with open arms.

For the next few years, life at home was hell. My mom was barely at home and when she did come home, she yelled at us about everything. This is why I stayed as busy as humanly possible.

My middle school years flew by and before I knew it, it was time to move on to high school. I was excited. Mostly because the three major Kentwood middle schools combined to one high school and I was told that all of the fine boys went to the other schools. I was looking forwarding to seeing new faces.

The school I went to had a campus building just for freshmen and a building across the parking lot for 10-12 graders. Occasionally, we found some reason to make our way to the 10-12 building but for the most part, all 700 plus of us freshmen hung out in our building.

I must say, my freshman year was the best year of my adolescent life. First off, the first week was so much fun.

I would never consider myself a player but by the third day of school I had four different guys trying to get with me. My cellphone was blowing up and I had so many letters to write back, I had to take them home to finish. Passing notes was the thing back when I was in grade school.

You couldn't tell me nothing!

I stayed with my hair done, I had all of the newest Jordans and Forces and my clothes were always on point.

On top of that, I was a cheerleader.

Your girl was doing her thang!

After the hype wore off, I found myself still attracted to one of the four guys that was interested in me. He was a basketball player. And in my 14-year-old eyes, he was the finest boy I had ever seen. His fly matched my fly and he was smart. I knew this because while most of us were taking Algebra he was taking Geometry in the 10-12 building.

I found comfort in spending time with him. Walking to and from class, talking on the phone and kissing after practice.
The harsh reality of my home life disappeared whenever I was with him.

I also found comfort in hanging with my girls on the weekends. Almost every weekend I would convince my mom to let me stay the night over one of my friend's house or to let them stay at ours.

Despite my mom not being home much she still tried her best to be a responsible parent. She made it a point to meet my friends' parents and when she couldn't meet them, she would at least talk to them on the phone.

One weekend, I asked to spend the night over one of my really good friend's house. I had stayed the night over her house before, so my mom didn't feel the need to meet her mom again.

My friend's mom had gone out of town and we had the house to ourselves. We thought it would be a great idea to invite some boys over and drink.

Before this night, I had never gotten drunk. I can't remember how we got our hands on some liquor but before I knew it, I was sitting on the bedroom floor in a daze.

I had just finished a whole bottle of beer, my best friend was telling me a story, but I couldn't react.

All I could do was stare at her.

After a while, she started calling my name.

"Keoshia, Keoshia!"

I could not move.

"Keoshia!" She slapped my leg.

It was almost as if her slapping my leg brought me back to planet earth. I refocused my attention and started cracking up laughing.

I was as drunk as a skunk. It took everything in me to try to stand up. Once I was standing, my whole body was tingling.

As I was trying to describe how I felt, my friends were cracking up laughing at me.

I joined them in laughter as I attempted to walk around the room.

Believe it or not, I was having a blast. I couldn't walk straight, and I kept having to go to the bathroom, but everything was 10 times funnier and I was having a good time with my friends.

The next day, I called my brother to come pick me up.

This was a perk of having an older brother.

Whenever I did not want to face my mother after a night of doing something, I had no business doing, I would call my brother. Despite us not having the best relationship he always came through.

For a small fee of course.

At the time gas was extremely cheap so I could offer him $5 in gas money, and he'd come pick me up with no problem. He would even let me drive his car if I put the gas back in it.

In a sense, our delinquency brought us closer together. He would use me to open the patio door whenever he would sneak out of the house and I would use him to pick me up or take me places behind our mom's back.

I remember one night my friends and I went to a house party. A girl that attended our school was throwing a party while her mom was out of town.

Side Note: If I ever have children, I will never ever ever leave them at home alone while I am out of town.

There were so many people at the party including my boyfriend. We were having the time of our lives drinking, talking and laughing.

My best friend and I had caught a ride with a random girl that she had just met the day before. The girl had come from out of town and was ready to go back home. I was not ready to leave. So, I stayed at the party with my boyfriend and his friends. I told my best friend I would call her when I was on my way back to her house.

The funny thing about being drunk is you have no sense of time. Somehow it was 3AM and I was just leaving the party.

"Hey, I'm outside," I said to my friend on the phone.

"Come to the back."

I stumbled to the back of the house.
When I got inside the house her grandma was sitting at the table with disappointment written all over her face.

I was so drunk all I kept thinking to myself was "Why didn't they just let me in the front door?"

We sat in silence for what felt like forever. My head was spinning and all I wanted to do was go to bed.

"Call your mother to have her come pick you up," demanded her grandma.

"She's out of town," I lied.

After spending a few more minutes trying to get information from me about my mom and her phone number, my friend's grandma gave up and let us go to bed.

The next day I woke up as early as I possibly could and called my brother to come and pick me up.

When I saw him pull up, I hurried to the car and told him to pull off as soon as I got in.

My friend's grandma was heading toward the car to try to tell on me and I wasn't haven't it.

I told my brother a much milder version of the story so that if he did try to tell our mom what happened, I wouldn't get in that much trouble.

You would think that after a night like that I would have gotten my act together but that was fuel to my fire. I was on a roll to have as much drunken fun as I could with my girls.

For the rest of the school year, we made sure we were at all of the parties including some of the college parties.

We quickly became known as the life of the party. Not to be dramatic but the parties literally got better when we walked in and if we weren't there people would call and ask us to show up.

Chapter 3
The Divorce

Even with all of the partying I did as a freshman, I somehow still managed to finish the year with a 4.0 GPA.

I moved on to my sophomore year as an honor roll student and Varsity Cheerleader. On top of this, I had moved up in rank at my dance studio, I was now dancing at the competitive level.

I was living my best life!

My ninth-grade boyfriend and I were still together but we were long distance.

Crazy, Right?!

Over the summer he got caught sneaking out the house, so his grandma shipped him off to Indiana to live with his dad. Even though we had no idea how it would work out, we committed to staying together. We emailed each other frequently and talked on the phone when we could. He didn't have a cellphone back then.

School started back up for the 2005/2006 school year. After the wild summer we had, you would have thought that my friends and I were ready to chill out. I'd say our partying and hanging out did decrease from 100% to about 80%.

On top of going to school I was cheering, dancing, trying to maintain a long-distance relationship and working at McDonald's, I did not have as much time to party.

Apparently, when you demonstrate your intelligence by getting a 4.0 GPA, your academic counselor and teachers think it's a good idea to put you in advance classes.

Looking back, I appreciate them for pushing me to take those classes, but at the time it meant that school required more focus. It also meant that I would no longer have classes with any of my friends.

My sophomore year was all about learning to balance. I was literally living a double life.

Studying like a nerd through the week and partying like a wild child on the weekends.

By now you would think my home life had improved but things were only getting worse. At this point, my mom and stepdad's marriage was over but every time my mom would try to put my stepdad out he would threaten her.

One day she came home and packed all of his belongings into black garbage bags and put them outside on the street curb.

That night he came home banging on the door.

She had changed the lock on the door, so he could not get in. For about 15 minutes he yelled like a crazy man outside as he banged on the door.

"Let me in!!" he yelled. "I will set the house on fire if you do not open the door!"

He finally stopped so we thought the worst was over.

"Boom!"

A loud noise sounded from downstairs. We ran down the stairs to the side door and there he was standing in the doorway. He had kicked the door in.

Without thought, I took off running upstairs, my mom right behind me. She grabbed my brother out of his room and we locked ourselves in her room. We sat there in silence for a few minutes.

"Recee" my stepdad called to my mom as he tried opening the bedroom door. "Why are you doing this?"

"I want a divorce!" my mom screamed.

And just like that, he was gone. He had finally agreed to the divorce that my mom had been begging for.

That night I sat on my bed for hours crying. My stepdad had given me a teddy bear that contained a music box inside of it. For hours I twisted the spindle over and over.

I was sad. I mean, I was happy my mom would no longer have to put up with him, but I was sad because he meant a lot to me.

I didn't have the best relationship with my own father so my stepdad sort of filled the void and now that void was left wide open yet again.

Like many other young girls who grow up without a strong father figure, I looked to fill that void through dating guys and partying with my friends.

Once the divorce was finalized things slowly got better at home. Although my mom still worked a lot, she was nicer and easier to talk to.

But by then, I was already waist-deep into partying so, the fun continued.

We were having one of our regular weekend shindigs. My favorite adult cousins were in town and my two best friends were over our house.

By this point, my mom knew that I had drank alcohol before, but I don't think she was fully aware of how much and how often I was drinking.

Anyway, my adult cousin had made me a drink. I took the drink upstairs to my room and shared it with my friends.

We started feeling a slight buzz and decided we need to get out of the house.

My homegirl called a few of our other friends and they were all over our homeboy's house. My boyfriend was there too so you know I had to figure out a way to get out of the house. His grandma had let him move back a few weeks into the school year.

I asked my mom if we could go over there. I told her his mom was letting him have a few people over. The truth is his mom wasn't even home. But my brother had already agreed to take us and pick us up, so I didn't have anything to worry about.

"I need to speak with his mother." said my mom when I asked her.

"Houston, we have a problem!" I thought to myself.

I went back upstairs to brainstorm with my friends. One of my friends knew all of the tricks, so she came up with the master plan.

She knew a girl our aged that had a mature voice. We called her and explained that we needed her to act like she was our guy friend's mom.
It worked!

On our way out the door, my cousin slipped me another drink.

When we got to our homeboy's house there were about 10 of our other friends hanging out outside of the house.

For a while we sat around talking, cracking jokes and laughing. But it wouldn't be worth telling this story if something crazy didn't happen, right?

After about an hour or so of just hanging out someone pulled up with a fifth of Everclear 190-proof Vodka.

The guys that brought it were really hyped up about it.

They were talking about how strong it is, but this meant nothing to me. In my mind, I was a pro at drinking.

We blessed the bottle (a tradition in which everyone touches the bottle before opening it), opened it, and started passing it around.
Every time someone took a sip, the crowd made a big commotion about it. When the bottle got to me everyone was telling my boyfriend not to let me drink any.
"Man, she got it." He told them.

This was all the encouragement I needed to down a big gulp.

"You didn't even drink that much." Several people commented after I drank from the bottle.

"Here let me see." I grabbed the bottle and starting drinking more."

I don't know why I was trying to be so tough; my throat and chest were burning so bad.

Literally two seconds after drinking it, I was drunker than I had ever been.

I cannot remember everything clearly, but I do recall everyone trying to influence me and my boyfriend to have sex.

People were always trying to get us to have sex. They would tease us and try to stick us in a room together to see what we would do. Almost, always we would just sit and talk. Sometimes we kissed but it didn't go much past that.

That night, our "friends" were really pressuring us. Next thing I know we were in the back of a car, my pants were off, and my panties were in my hand.

While we were kissing, we noticed police lights coming from behind the car. I hurried up and pulled my pants up and jumped out of the car.

When I realized my underwear were still in my hand I just put them in my pocket.

Surprisingly we didn't get in trouble. The officer just told us we had to go home because they received a call about a noise disturbance. My boyfriend and I got in the car with a few of his guy friends. I had no idea where my homegirls had gone but I figured we would link up at the next destination.

We really didn't have anywhere to go so we just road around for a minute. While we were riding around my boyfriend's aunt called him and told him he had to come home.

When we pulled up to his house, I was sad. I really didn't want him to go. I got out of the car to give him a hug.

I don't know if he was trying to show out in front of his friends or what, but he started rubbing all over my butt and kissing me with a lot of passion. His friends were making all sorts of comments to the point where I really didn't want to get back in the car, but I had no one else to ride with.

As soon as I got in the car I texted my friends to find out where they were.

We headed over to one of their boyfriend's house.

On the ride over, the boy that was sitting in the back seat with me was trying to get my attention. I was trying my best to ignore him, but he moved closer. He put his hand on my thigh and started rubbing up and down. I pushed his hand away and he stopped.

When we got to the house. I kept telling myself to get out of the car, but my body wouldn't move.

There were three guys in the car, and they were making sexual comments toward me.

I'm not sure if it was fear or what but I made my way out of the car. The only problem was I could barely walk. I took a few steps and fell to the ground.
I laid there for what felt like hours, starring at the stars unable to move thinking about everything that had transpired minutes before.

I needed to get home. I didn't want my mom to see us like this.

Apparently, I was thinking too hard because the next thing I know she was calling my phone. This was enough motivation to get me off the ground.

I didn't answer the phone, but I got up and went looking for my friends.

When I found them, they were inside the house with their tongues down some boys' throats.

"Y'all we gotta go. We gotta get back to the house." I said to get their attention.

They both started laughing.

"Forreal, come on. My mom called, and I need to call her back but she's going to want to know where we are."

"Where exactly are we?" I asked.

It felt like we were in the middle of nowhere but turns out we were about 5 minutes away from the guy's house that we started at that night.

Once we got back to the house, I put on my best sober voice and called my mom back.

"Hello."

"I'm on my way to come get you." my mom said.

"What happened to Jefrey (my brother)? He was supposed to pick us up."

"He got pulled over."

I could have died.

Everything was going just fine until my mom said she was coming to get me. I figured we would just go behind the house and when she called we would come from behind the house as if we had been there the whole time.

Good plan, right?

Wrong!

When she pulled up. She got out of the car. My friends and I walked toward her to get in the car.

"Which house did y'all just come from?" my mom asked with anger in her voice.

I pointed to the house we had just come from. I could tell she had been drinking because she was being really angry and aggressive.

Two drunk people trying to figure things out is not a good idea.

She started walking toward the back of the house.

I was going to let her carry on, but I knew that was a waste of time.

I mumbled something under my breath. I can't remember what I said but knowing me it was something smart. I bent down to tie my shoe and out of nowhere, my mom started running toward me. I stood up but not before she could grab me by my hair.

She loosened her grip on my hair but still had my jacket. While she was gripping me up, she was yelling. I was still pretty drunk, so I don't know what she was saying but I knew I needed to get loose.

I unzipped my jacket and took off running down the street. I could hear her running after me. I also heard the sound of small rocks scraping the ground.

When I got a little bit down the street, I saw a couple of my homeboys hiding on the side of a neighbor's house. I walked over to them.

"Ke, yo mom fell," they both said.

"What?"

"Yeah, she fell when she was trying to catch you."

Next thing I know, my cousins were yelling my name.

"Ke, we need to get to the hospital." Where are you? We need to get your mom to the hospital, she fell."

I came from the side of the house and walked back to the car. When I got to the car door, I saw my mom sitting in the front seat with a shirt up to her mouth. Blood was everywhere. I started crying hysterically. I could not believe I had done this to my mom.

On the ride home, my mom was talking to me about how I need to make better decisions and watch who I am hanging out with. I could hear her, but my thoughts were overpowering her words.

I just couldn't believe I had hurt my mom in such a way that she was bleeding and needing to go to the hospital. I had seen her go through so much and here I was adding to the pain.

When we got home, my friends and I went up to my room and went to bed.

The next several months were strange.

Before the accident my mom and I had a pretty good relationship. I didn't tell her everything, but I spent a lot of time around her and I knew I could talk to her whenever I really needed to.

After the accident, our conversations were short.

Maybe it was because she was in too much pain to open her mouth or maybe it was because she was disappointed in me. Whatever it was, our relationship was damaged.

I tried apologizing, but things were still weird.

I stopped hanging with everyone that was out with me that night. I even stopped speaking to them at school. The only person I talked to was my boyfriend. This went on for months. I felt so alone but I didn't feel like I had a right to complain.

After all, it was my poor decision making that lead me to this place.

Chapter 4
Transitions

The last couple of years of high school were much less dramatic than the first two. By now many of the people I hung out with had been expelled from my high school. Also, I was taking harder classes such as Physics, Anatomy, AP Chemistry and Accounting. This meant I really had to focus on my schoolwork, no more playing around.

I still hung out on the weekends, but it was rare and when I did I was usually somewhere hugged up with my boyfriend.

Despite him going to a different school, we held on strong up until a few months before graduation.

He broke up with me because he said he needed to focus. He and I both knew this wasn't true and the fact that he had a new girlfriend a few weeks after, was my proof.

At the time, I was hurt to my core. I thought the world was coming to an end. Obviously, that wasn't true. Life went on just fine. I did, however, start back hanging out and partying with my friends. I needed a distraction from the pain plus no boo meant I had more time on my hands.

Even though I started back partying my grades remained good and I had been accepted into all six of the colleges I had applied to.

I was going to be a first-generation college student, so I had no clue which school to pick. My cousin promised me $100 if I went to the University of Michigan.

Off to U of M, I went!

My freshman year was rough. I only knew one person out of the thousands of other students. For about a month I contemplated transferring to Grand Valley State University, so I could be closer to home.

Believe it or not I had a four year, full-ride scholarship to go there. At the time I didn't know much about student debt. Plus, I was told the University of Michigan was a better school. In hindsight, I personally don't think it would have made a huge difference.

Guess I will never know.

One thing I do know is that my mom helped me make it through and if nothing else, attending the University of Michigan restored my mom and I's relationship. So much so that to this day she is my best friend.

It wasn't long before I found my niche. I started participating in a student-led organization called Sister to Sister. I also joined a dance team known as Climax. Many of the ladies in Sister to Sister also danced for Climax so we spent a lot of time together. Along with that was the fact that most of the girls were older.

You know what that means!?!

Access to liquor.

Having drank so much in high school, I was a bit more advanced than even the older girls.

Nevertheless, we had a great time anytime we hung out.

On one of our regular night outings to our only campus club, Studio Four, a bunch of us met up to pregame.

We would always pregame before we went out. First, because most of us were under 21 and second, because showing up to the party drunk was always better than buying drinks at the bar.

Makes sense, right?

Well, usually this was the best way to do it but on this particular night, I think we overdid ourselves.

As soon as we walked into the club the liquor hit.

Boom!

I was drunk out of my mind.

We danced for a little bit, but I found myself barely able to stand on my two feet, so I sat down on a bench against the wall. Soon after, my homegirl came and sat near me.

Drunkenly she said, "I have to go to the bathroom."

Despite, how drunk I was I made my way to the bathroom with her.

As soon as we entered the stall, she started throwing up in the toilet.

I guess we were in the stall too long because next thing I know I heard a man's voice.

"Is everything ok in there?" the man said.

"Yes, we will be out in a minute," I responded.

I gave my girl the pep talk and told her to pull it together.

She got up and we headed out of the stall.

Turns out the man was a club bouncer. He was not convinced that she was okay, and he took it upon himself to pick my friend up and carry her out of the club.

On our way out of the club, a girl called my friend a drunk B*&@$. I gave that girl a piece of my mind and carried on right behind the bouncer out of the door.

Thank goodness it was not cold outside, or we would have frozen to death.

Somehow, we made our way back inside the building to find our friends and leave.

To this day I still don't know how I made it back to my dorm room, but I did, and we all survived the night.

My freshman year was quite the year. It was a year of finding myself and finding my place where I fit in life.

On top of finding my niche with the student organization and dance group I also started attending a weekly bible study which lead me to start attending a nearby church.

As I mentioned at the beginning of this book, I knew of God, but I didn't really know God.

As I began to deepen my understanding of who God is and who I am in Christ, I began to see my life as having meaning and value.

Naturally, as I spent more time attending church services as well as serving on the transportation, dance and praise team ministry, I spent less time hanging out. I also stopped hanging out because my college course work was hard. Don't get me wrong I had a fun freshman year, but college course work was no joke.

I spent the summer between my freshman and sophomore year back in Grand Rapids at my mom's house, working as a dietary aid at a residential assistant living center.

Not long after being home for the summer, I met a guy at work, and we started dating. Things were moving pretty fast and before I knew it we were calling each other boyfriend and girlfriend.

I am honestly dreading including this relationship in this book because there is no reason why things should have moved past us dating over the summer. But here goes nothing.
For the first year of our relationship, he lived in Grand Rapids and I lived in Ann Arbor.

The relationship was so stressful. We were always arguing about the dumbest stuff. By this time, I rarely, if ever hung out with my friends because I knew if I even thought about going out, my boyfriend and I would argue.

I spent most of my time alone in my apartment studying or talking on the phone. And if I wasn't at home I was at a church-related event, work, student organization meeting or at dance practice.

I guess this was a good thing, less time with my friends also meant less time drinking and partying.

But the reality is, I didn't actually deal with my issues. I was simply distracted by other things.

Usually, when we just cover up our issues instead of dealing with them, they find a way to come back.

And sometimes they come back worse than before.

Chapter 5
The Monster Returns

By the time I started my junior year I had decided on psychology as my major with a pre-dental focus. I had been planning a career as an Orthodontist since eight grade and although the classes were difficult I was pretty sure I still wanted to be a dentist.

My junior year was also the time when I agreed to let my then boyfriend come stay with me. He was living with his mother at the time and she needed him to move out. He didn't have any money and nowhere to go so I thought, "Why not let him move in, get on his feet and then help me with rent as soon as he gets established."
We didn't have the best relationship, but I considered him a friend and wanted to help him.

As time went on we had a few good days but tons of bad ones. He had finally started working and was going to school but relationship wise we were not doing well at all.

I couldn't go out with my friends because anytime I would try to go out my boyfriend would start an argument, so I just stayed home most of the time.

Toward the end of my junior year, I began having what I called an identity crisis.

The more I learned about God, the more I felt lost about who I was and where I was going. I started to feel like everything that I had planned for my future was based on my own desires and not on what God wanted for me, so I began to pray and fast for answers.

One thing God began to show me was that my boyfriend and I needed to split. I agreed with God, but I was too afraid of all the what-ifs.

What if I can't afford to live on my own? What if, he won't move out? Where will he go? If, I leave my name will still be on the lease and what if he doesn't pay the rent then my credit will be messed up?

So many questions were going through my head that I ignored God. I did, however, break up with my boyfriend and encouraged him to sleep on the couch but I didn't put him out and I didn't move out.

This probably sounds crazy but for the remainder of my college experience, I lived in the house and slept in the bed with a man I was no longer in a relationship with.

On top of dealing with relationship issues, God was showing me that he had a different plan for my career. I had been considering getting a dual degree in dentistry and public health but the more I prayed about it, the more I felt I was being pulled toward only pursuing a Master of Public Health.

The what-ifs began to creep up again but instead of wondering what my life would be like if I changed my career path I decided to trust God. I figured I was going to have to trust him with something. I was one class away from completing all of my pre-dental requirements when I walked into the counseling center to drop the class. As soon as I dropped the class I felt more peace than I had ever felt. I did not know what the future would hold but I was ready for the ride.

Well, at least I thought I was.

I graduated college and headed to Little Rock, Arkansas in July 2012 for a yearlong service project.

You may be wondering why in the world would I move to Little Rock, Arkansas?

I had a choice between there and many other more popular cities, but I picked Arkansas because my family had history there. Both my grandparents and their parents had been born and raised near Little Rock and so I felt it would be a great opportunity to learn more about my family background.

The first few months were great! Although we worked long 10-hour days, we had fun at work and we even got together on the weekends. We would go out, have little parties at each other's apartments and even take weekend trips to nearby cities.
Not too long into the year though, things started to change.

Those 10-hour workdays became stressful and filled with drama. And instead of enjoying being around my coworkers, all I wanted to do was be alone.

On top of the work stress, life began to hit me hard as I had my first encounter with the "real world".

I had heard adults talk about this "real world" concept while I was in college, but I often brushed it off.

I'd think to myself, "This is the real world! I pay my own bills and I am independent."

The truth is, I knew nothing about the real world.

By November, I had run out of money from my savings account.

I was making about $6/hour with a $500 a month rent plus an additional $100-150 for utilities. To top it off, the engine on my car went out. I had no social network or resources to ask for help and I was broke!

About a week after I opened a credit card to pay $2000 for a new engine, someone ran a red light and totaled my car. I was grateful to have made it through the accident without any harm to my body, but truth be told I was over it. I just couldn't believe this was my life after college.

I was completely lost.

My mom did what she could to support me but she was 10 hours away so there was only so much that she could do.

So here I was, in debt, barely making ends me, in need of a new car, with no real friends or support system.

I did what I knew how to do best.

Drink.

For the first time in my years of drinking, I began drinking alone. I went from drinking socially, to drinking to get through my stress. After work, I would go home to sit in my one chair to watch the same DVDs over and over until I crashed on my blowup mattress.

Then I'd wake up to do it all over again the next day.

I was going to church. I was even singing in the choir, but I didn't have enough sense to call on God. Honestly, I could barely pray. Someone must have been praying for me though.

Within a couple of weeks after the accident, I ended up finding a second job that was flexible with my current work schedule. And, somehow, I got a new car with zero down and a super low, affordable car payment.

I have thanked God before but as I write, I cannot help but have tears in my eyes. God was so good to me during this time.

I didn't deserve it.

I wasn't living my life to honor him and yet he still loved me enough to pour his favor over my life. If God has ever shown you favor, just take a second to thank him!

Despite experiencing this hardship, I was able to complete the program with a stronger sense of who I was and what I was capable of achieving.

My experience in Little Rock helped me to develop the character and strength I needed to get through the next two years.

I left Little Rock and went on to graduate school at Drexel University in Philadelphia.

I thought living alone in Arkansas was something until I got to Philadelphia. I traded $500 a month rent for $800 a month rent. And for the first month, I lived in an apartment infested with mice and roaches. I literally thought I was going to die.

Nevertheless, this was lightweight compared to what I had gone through in Little Rock.

Although I did not love living in Philly, I was comfortable. I was focused on school and my physical fitness. I even had a small group of friends that I enjoyed hanging out with occasionally.
I was still a pretty heavy drinker though. Maybe even more at this time than before.

One thing about college, especially graduate school was that they tend to have a lot of social networking events. And for some reason, we always received free drink tickets. More often than not, I would have 4-5 free drinks at these events. I didn't have much willpower when it came to free food and free drinks, so I took full advantage of both.

Living in a big city for the first time meant visitors. Understandably, no one wanted to visit me when I lived in Little Rock but now that I was in Philly my homegirls wanted to visit and experience the big city living.

I found a club that would allow us to have a 1-hour open bar, a bottle of champagne and VIP seating for just $100. This was a deal we couldn't beat! So, for my 25th birthday, I planned a birthday weekend to remember. Or should I say, try to remember?

When all my girls arrived, we spent the first couple of hours getting something to eat and then of course drinking and getting ready for the party.

I had put together a special spiked punch that had tons of liquor but tasted like juice.

Turns out it was one of those drinks that sneak up on you when you least expect it.

For a couple of hours, we sipped on the punch while getting dressed and taking pictures. Then we headed out to the club.

Some of my girls had never road the subway so that was interesting.

One of my friends, who has been my homegirl since high school, had us dying laughing on the subway. She was standing up acting like she was surfing, talking to strangers and just being the complete goofy girl, she is known to be.

The ride to the club was one of the best parts of the night.

Once we got to our stop, we made our way to the club. It was 11PM.

We were supposed to get there at 10PM if we wanted to partake in the 1-hour open bar. I guess I didn't realize how much time it takes 8 girls to get ready.
Anyway, we rushed to the door and made our way inside. Leave it up to my goofy, friendly, bestfriend to get us free drinks to make up for our missed open bar hour.

Despite us not needing anything else to drink, we drank the free drinks and headed to the dance floor.

While dancing I fell.

SMH!

I had never been so drunk in public that I fell.
I played it off pretty good though. At least, I felt like I did.

Once I fell, I started dancing on the floor.

What made it funny was that one of Beyoncé's sexy songs was playing so it was almost like I was trying to remake one of her videos.

But regardless of how good I played it off, I am pretty sure I looked a hot mess. I was so embarrassed that once I figured out a way to get up, I took off straight to the bathroom.

I felt sick to my stomach and needed to get out of there quick!

When I left out of the bathroom, I headed over to our VIP table to find my friends.

"Y'all, it's time to go!"

"We just got here!!" they said.

"I know but I don't feel well, we need to go now!" I shouted over the music.

I felt so bad asking them to leave after we had already gotten there late and hadn't even been there for more than an hour but there was no way I could stay there another minute. If they wanted me to be able to walk on my own two feet we had to leave immediately.

We took a taxi back to my place.

As soon as we got back to my apartment, I headed straight to the toilet.

I was being a terrible host because my girls had no idea where anything was, and I couldn't even help them.

After I threw up everything I had eaten for the past two days, I was back to normal. I came out of the bathroom to find just one of my friends still in the apartment.

Apparently, the other ones had found some random guys to go smoke weed with.

I called them to make sure they were ok.

"What are y'all doing? Where y'all at?" I asked

"We next door at Rally's smoking in the parking lot. Come over here."
"I'm good." I'll see y'all when y'all come up.

I had had enough for the night. Plus, I wasn't a smoker. I had smoked weed a few times before but quickly decided that wasn't my thing.

About an hour later, they came knocking on my door talking and laughing loudly.

All I could do was laugh with them.

This was one crazy night but thankfully it ended with us all sound asleep, safe!

Chapter 6
It's Time to Quit

"I want to stop drinking" ~journal entry I wrote July 17, 2015.

I spent one more year in Philadelphia. After graduating I headed off to New York City. I have no idea why I thought I would like NYC when I had already determined I wasn't a big city girl but there I was living in Harlem and working in the Bronx.

I had taken a fellowship position at a community health center in the Bronx.

The fellowship turned out to be much different than what I had expected, and I began to experience great discontentment.

To help, I thought it would be a good idea for my boyfriend at the time to come live with me. This was a new boyfriend that I had met while I was living in Philadelphia.

You're probably thinking "This girl stayed with a boyfriend!"

It's true. I stayed with a man. It never failed.

Anytime I would commit to being single I would find myself another relationship.

Anyway, I figured the distance was adding to the disappointment and sadness I was feeling so I asked him to move in with me.

Things started off great! We explored the city together and overall was having a good time. But after a couple of months, my work stress and his life stress started to conflict. The more time we spent together the more I realized we were not a good fit. We stopped enjoying each other and every time we talked we were having a conversation about problems that needed to be fixed either in my life, his life or in our relationship.

The unhappier I was with my job and relationship, the more I looked for an escape. I was trying my hardest not to turn to the bottle for relief so instead, I flew home to Michigan at least once a month.

Eventually, my boyfriend moved out and I ran out of money to travel to Michigan.

With no escape, I started back drinking. I found myself at the liquor store every other day.

It got to a point where I started to feel embarrassed about how much I was drinking so I started hiding the bottles in my room so that my roommates did not see them.

For about 5 months I went to work, came home to watch Netflix on my laptop and drink wine.

I rarely went anywhere and when I did, I was most likely hanging out with other people who were drinking.

I even started having dreams of doing cocaine.

Thank God I never actually tried it.

I was so down, depressed, unmotivated and uninspired that I was running out of hope.

I began wondering what was the point of living.

With so much hopelessness inside of me, I started trying to pray and read the bible.

But no matter how hard I tried; I couldn't pray.

When praying I would either get distracted with my thoughts or something would come up in the middle of me praying. And whenever I tried to read the word, the words on the page would look like gibberish.

It felt like nothing was working to save me from my misery.

All I could do was count the days that I would be done with the fellowship which I hoped would bring back my sense of peace and joy.

I don't know how but I made it to the end of the fellowship program and was heading to Tanzania, Africa.

One of the only reasons I did not quit the fellowship was because I knew that at the end of the year, they were going to fly us to Africa for a one week, all expenses paid, trip.

So as much as I hated the experience, I really really really wanted to go on the trip.

Side Note: There is nothing. I mean absolutely nothing, that is worth losing your peace and sanity over. God graced me to make it through that experience but if I could have done it over, I would have passed up that free trip to protect my mind from the hell I went through.

If it costs you your peace, it is too expensive
~Unknown

As soon as we checked into our hotel, a friend of mine and I headed straight for the liquor store.

There was a small-town liquor store about a 10-minute walk from the hotel we were staying at, so we walked.

It was quite interesting walking around on an entirely different continent for the first time.

We walked the streets like we were natives to the town.

That is until we got to the store and the man did not speak a lick of English. Things got even more interesting when he did not give us back the right amount of change.

Somehow someway through sign language and broken English, I was able to get the man to understand that he owed me more money back.

The fact that the very first thing I did was find a liquor store tells me I had a problem.

But it wasn't until I woke up in my hotel room at 3AM in the morning with clothes everywhere and broken glass on the bathroom floor that I began to reevaluate my life.

I had no idea how I had gotten back to my room.

The last thing I remembered was sitting poolside, laughing and talking with the other people from the fellowship program.

After cleaning up my room, I took a shower and fell back to sleep. I ended up sleeping until about noon the next day.
When I woke up I looked in the refrigerator. I had a fifth of Absolut Vodka and all that was left was ¼ of the bottle. I couldn't believe I had drunk that much liquor by myself. I was surprised I was still alive.

I poured out the rest of the bottle.

This was the first of many attempts at quitting.

That day, I spent the rest of the day sitting on the balcony, staring at the ocean, reflecting on life. I thought about the past, present, and future.

I reflected on the fellowship experience and began to think about my goals for the year to come. Prior to this trip, I hadn't had the time or mental compacity to plan anything.

I knew for certain I wanted to move back to Michigan. I also knew that it was time for me to stop drinking. But what I did not know is, how?

All I ever knew was drinking.

I had no idea how to actually stop drinking. I wasn't even confident I would be able to stop. Believe it or not, I didn't know anyone who had never drank alcohol. And I only knew two people that had drank before but no longer did, my friend I met in graduate school and my mom's new husband.

After the retreat, my friend and I spent one more week in Africa. We went on a Safari in Tanzania and spent that last few days in Zanzibar.

Side Note: If you have never been to Africa you absolutely need to go at least once! The experience is life-changing.

When I arrived back to the States, I moved back to Grand Rapids, MI.

While in Grand Rapids I lived a lowkey lifestyle.

Having just gotten through a really tough year in NYC, I did not have much energy. I spent my days filling out job applications, substitute teaching and trying to restore my relationship with my boyfriend.

Things were still rocky with us.

It was almost like no matter what we tried; we could not get things back the way they used to be. Quite frankly, the more we tried the worse things would get.

I thought that once I had moved back to Michigan life would get better and that my relationship would improve as well as my drinking problem.

Neither situation changed.

Looking back, I realize that my problem was not external it was internal and that no matter what I changed on the outside, I would continue to struggle in those areas until I fixed what was on the inside.

The unfortunate part is that I had no idea how to change the inside. I just knew that I did not like what I saw when I looked in the mirror. Not the physical features but the inside. When I looked in the mirror I could see hurt and pain in my eyes.

After a few months in Grand Rapids with no luck on finding a permanent job, I started applying for jobs outside of the city.

Within no time I had received a call to interview for a position in Saginaw, MI. The interviewing panel was so impressed that they offered me the job.

I packed up my bags yet again and was heading off to another new city. Well, not so much a "new" city.

I was born in Saginaw and lived in the city until I was six.

Surprisingly I remember quite a bit about my childhood in Saginaw.

I was born at Saginaw General Hospital, February 4, 1990. It was my brother's birthday and my mom had planned a party for him. I wasn't due for another week, but God had a different plan.

Maybe this is the real reason my brother and I didn't get along growing up; I ruined his 2nd birthday party.

When I was a child living in Saginaw, things seemed perfect from the outside looking in.

We had both of our parents in our lives, we never needed anything, and we had a nice house with several cars. We even had a dog. All we were missing is the white picket fence.

It's funny how material things can hide the truth.

The truth was our home was broken.

My dad was rarely home.

Sometimes when he was home he would sit me on his lap and sing to me. These were the moments I loved the most, but those moments were few and far in between. More often than not when my dad was home, he was sleep, counting money or arguing with my mom.

One night while my brother and I were sleeping, I heard a loud boom. The noise was so loud that it scared me out of my sleep. I ran to my brother's room, but he laid their sleep. I ran back into my room, grabbed my cover and ran back into his room.

I spent the night sleeping on my brother's bedroom floor. This was my go-to spot anytime I was afraid.

The next morning my mom came into the room to wake us up for school.

Everything seemed normal until I got downstairs and noted that the dining room table was shattered all over the floor. The frame to the table and the chairs remained in place but the entire glass piece was broken into little pieces all over the floor and so was my heart.

This wasn't the first time my parents had gotten into it and it definitely was not the last.

My mom finally found the strength to leave.

While my dad was locked up, my mom used the opportunity to escape. She moved to Grand Rapids, MI while my brother and I stayed behind and lived with my grandmother for a year.

It was hard living away from my mom, but my grandma did a really good job raising us. She did what grandmas do best, she spoiled us rotten.

Once, my mom got herself settle in Grand Rapids, my brother and I moved with her. The day I moved from Saginaw; I was certain that I would never return. Maybe to visit but definitely not to live.

God sure does have a way of making us laugh!

Chapter 7
Finding My Peace

The first few months of living in Saginaw were a little rough. If I haven't made it clear by now, let me make it known, I do not do well with transitions. Everything about transitioning makes me uncomfortable.

On top of being in a new space where I didn't know anyone, my boyfriend and I finally decided to cut our ties.

Even though I saw it coming and we both knew it was necessary, it hurt really bad.

I was so tired of being hopeful about relationships only for them to end in disappointment.

Pain from the breakup and boredom from living in a city with no friends meant after work was time for wine and home remodeling.

Turns out drinking and remodeling are not a good combination. One night I almost cut my finger off. There was blood everywhere.

Thankfully I didn't have to go to the hospital and it healed quickly.

Although things started off rough, I began to enjoy living in Saginaw.

When I first moved I figured I'd live in Saginaw for a few months until I heard back from one of the positions I had applied for in Grand Rapids. But the more time I spent in Saginaw the more I began to experience peace and joy like I'd never experienced them before.

I found my niche pretty quickly. I had a couple of people at work that I felt comfortable hanging out with outside of work.

I also started coaching cheerleading and exercising regularly. On top of that, I started back going to church.

I had finally reached a place in my life where everything around me was quiet enough that I could finally hear my own thoughts and begin to heal from my past.

Who would have thought that the very place that birthed my pain, was the same place God would use to set me free!

Don't get me wrong, I still struggled with drinking, but one thing is for sure, I became more aware of who I was created to be. God began to show me that my life had purpose and meaning beyond what I could understand. I began to explore the root causes of my addiction and started to heal from all of the trauma.

One evening, my aunt and I were having a conversation and she said, "Everything a person decides to do is a choice." I questioned her statement by asking "What about people who become alcoholics because their parents are alcoholics?"

She stood firm in her belief that even then, it is still a choice.

After some thought, I agreed with her. It is true. Deciding to drink is a choice but what happens when the power to choose is taken.

My power to choose whether or not I wanted to become a drinker was taken away from me at a very early age.

I was trained to be a drinker.

Michael Todd, the Lead Pastor of Transformation Church, delivered a sermon titled Daddy Issues-All Strings Attached (Part I). It can be found on YouTube if you are interested in watching the whole message.

In the message, he speaks on this very idea of train up a child. He firmly states that everything we do, we were taught.

I was taught how to drink my problems away. I was taught how to turn to alcohol to find temporary peace. I learned to use drinking as a way to fit in with people around me. I learned that when you get together with family and friends there needed to be food and alcohol to make it a good time.

In the video after he read Proverbs 22:6 to his congregation, Pastor Todd poses several questions. "What if you were trained wrong?" "Who trained you?" "Are you still attached to their training.?"

I was trained in the way of drinking, but I reached a point where I wanted to depart from that training.

I got tired of driving home intoxicated hoping I'd make it home without getting into an accident or getting pulled over. I got tired of coming home from work not being able to be productive because I was too tipsy to think or function. I got tired of showing up to evening bible study feeling paranoid because I thought someone might smell the alcohol on my breath.

Drinking was getting in the way of my physical, mental and spiritual growth and I had had enough.

I finally understood that it was going to take more than just wanting to stop drinking to stop.

It was going to take some fasting, some praying and some deep soul searching.

The change wasn't going to happen overnight.

I started by limiting my trips to the grocery store. When I would go to the store I would leave my driver's licenses at home.

I would also fast from drinking anything other than water.

Sometimes when I didn't have the will power to not buy liquor or when family members would leave liquor at my house. After a few drinks, I'd find myself pouring out mostly full bottles of wine trying my absolute hardest to stop drinking.

My goodness, the struggle was real!

It was even harder not to drink when I was with friends and family who I normally would drink around.

I didn't speak much about wanting to stop drinking because I didn't feel like people would understand. I also didn't feel like explaining how I reached this place in my life. I felt that people would judge me for my past or try to convince me that drinking wasn't that bad.

So instead of fully sharing what I was going through, I struggled alone. And the more I held it in that I was fighting this battle, the more I felt like I was losing.

One night, I decided to step out. I hadn't been out in a while and I was tired of always being in the house. I heard about a party happening at a club that I had been to once before.

I went solo dolo as I tend to do. I figured once I got there I'd run into someone I knew.

I didn't plan on drinking but when I got there, there were only three other people at the club, so I grabbed a drink at the bar, found a good seat, sat and drank while I people watched.

After about an hour the crowd started picking up and long and behold this guy I used to have a crush on walked in the door.

I hurried up and went to the bathroom.

I knew it was possible that he would be there, but I was hoping he wouldn't show up. I had quickly learned that he was a jerk and I really didn't want to see him.

When I came out of the bathroom I should have headed for the door but instead, I headed to the bar to get another drink.

I guess I called myself trying to stunt. I was cute, so I thought since I am here why not let him see me.

As I walked back to my seat, I spotted him. He was whispering in some woman's ear but looked up in my direction. You would have thought he had seen a ghost. I know he saw me, but he never approached me.

I wasn't tripping though, because I didn't come there for him.

After finishing my drink, I got on the dance floor.

I don't know what it is about music and dancing that heightens your buzz but next thing I knew I was barely able to stand up.

Men were coming at me left and right trying to dance and get my phone number. It was all a bit too much, so I snuck out.

I have no idea how I got home but when I woke up the next morning I was so disappointed in myself. So much so that I cried. I knew better, I wanted better and I was determined to do better.

The next day when I went to church the praise and worship team started singing *Just Want You* by Travis Greene. If you aren't familiar with the song, I recommend that you stop reading right now and listen to it. The song says, "Take everything, I don't want it, I don't need it, God…I just want you."

Those words began to penetrate my heart to the point where I found myself at the alter surrendering everything to God.

At that moment I prayed for God to take the desire to drink out of me. With my head down and hands slightly lifted, my mouth opened, and I begin to yell out. As I yelled, it felt as if I was throwing up, but nothing was coming out. It is difficult to explain but I believe God was literally taking the spirit of alcoholism out of my body.

When I got up from the alter, I knew something was different. God had allowed me to experience him in a way that I had never experienced him before. At that moment, I believe God began to transform me.

No longer did I have to try by my own willpower to stop drinking but I could lean on God to end this cycle.

Chapter 8:
Loose But Not Free

The months to follow were not easy. I found it difficult to tell other people that I had decided to stop drinking. I also begin to have doubts in my mind. I did not think I could actually maintain this change for the rest of my life.

When I would tell my friends and family that I had quit drinking, they would ask me why. I would say things like "I just don't want to drink anymore" or "It's not good to drink." But I would never tell them the real reason which was because God was taking me to a new level in my walk with him and he wanted me to walk in the fullness of who he created me to be.

I guess I was afraid of sounding too spiritual or having people ask me a bunch of questions relating to Christianity. I had had enough of the "Jesus turned water into wine" arguments.

Some readers may be thinking right now, "Isn't that true?"

It is true, but Jesus turning water into wine was not about him encouraging drinking wine. This was the first miracle Jesus performed and it was a demonstration of the old things (Old Testament) becoming new (New Testament).

I am not a bible scholar, so I won't go any deeper than that. The last thing I will say is always read the bible through the lens of the Holy Spirit, not your flesh, so that you can get the revelation of the text and not just the surface.

On top of people asking why I stopped drinking they would ask questions like, "Are you pregnant?" or "Do you mean for right now or FOREVER!?"

I even had people who I thought loved me, doubt me. They'd laugh it off, saying things like you will be back drinking by the time I see you again or we will see how long this lasts.

I did not find much support among my friends and family, so I found myself feeling pretty alone in the world.

The thing about stopping a habit like drinking is that you have to find a new way to do everything. A new way to relax, a new way to hang out with friends and family, a new way to eat dinner, etc.

It is so easy to fall back into a bad habit when temptation is all around you. Drinking is normalized in America to the point where no matter where you go, alcohol is present. Because of this, I had to pretty much isolated myself. If I wasn't at work, I was at church and if not, I was at home.

I had been going strong for three months.

About a year before deciding to stop drinking, I had planned a girls' trip to New Orleans (NOLA) for Essence Fest with my mom and her friends.

The last time I visited NOLA was for Mardi Gras and I was all the way LIT so that is what came to mind every time I thought about the city.

Also, the movie Girls Trip was based on a group of women who went to NOLA for Essence Fest and had the time of their lives. The best scenes in the movie were the ones where they were drinking and partying.

Knowing this, I decided to still go. I had already paid for my room, flight and concert tickets, plus I figured I was strong enough by then to not get tempted.

Boy oh boy was I fooling myself.

The first day was smooth. I woke up, read my word, meditated and listened to some good Gospel music.

I told myself "You got this!"

When we got to the concert my mom's friend grabbed some drinks. She handed me one. I hadn't told her that I had stopped drinking. I guess I was afraid of the judgment I had received from the times I had told people before.

I grabbed the drink and figured one wouldn't hurt.

Of course, I was wrong, I ended up having a few more drinks during the duration of my trip.

For the next seven months, temptation was limited because I kept to myself.

When I would go places where there was alcohol I would limit my time there. I would also, avoid the alcohol section of the grocery store. I didn't have it all figured out, but I knew that I was easily tempted so I had to protect myself as much as possible.

I thought I was delivered. I was passing up drinks left and right.

It was almost like I had gotten cocky. Not that I believed I had done something, but I figured God had magically removed the taste out of my mouth and that I was good to go.

Until one day, I came home, and my mom was visiting from out of town. She had a bottle of wine on the kitchen counter. I was feeling stressed, so I grabbed a small glass, poured a little and hurried up and drank it before anyone could see me.

I didn't feel a buzz or anything and to be honest, it was nasty, so I figured I was good.

However, days later I found myself craving wine. I started telling myself, "You're delivered from alcoholism, a little wine here and there won't hurt. I quickly found out that was not true.

Within 2 months, 1-2 occasional glasses of wine quickly turned into one bottle of wine 4-5 nights a week.

The night I drank my forever, last drink, I was reading notes out of one of my notebooks. I came across something my Pastor had spoken over me back in November (Nov 4, 2018, to be exact).

My Pastor had said to me "I see a strong drinking spirit in your family...it has been passed through your bloodline... God is going to bless you for breaking the generational curse. Get ready to rejoice! The issue is over. Drinking will no longer be a curse in your bloodline after you!"

At that moment I was reminded that this thing is much bigger than me and that if I want true long-term transformation for myself and for my family bloodline, I was going to have to make some real sacrifices.

One day, early June 2019, I was removing dead leaves from a plant. Most of them came off with ease but some I had to pull off and some I had to eventually cut off. They were clearly dead, but I couldn't get them off as easily.

This made me think about my life. I thought of myself as if I was the plant and drinking was the dead leaves. Being known as a drinker had died from my identity and it was time to cut it off. It was time to set a deadline for this behavior.

The type of deadline that says, "Enough is Enough." I was tired of going around the same mountain dealing with the same thing over and over. So, I decided that June 30, 2019, would be the deadline. I was willing to take on new challenges but after June 30th I was no longer willing to be defeated by alcoholism any longer.

I became intentional about preparing for this deadline.

First and foremost, I got back in God's presence. I started praying and fasting. This time was different than any other time.

Every day, I was intentional about reading the Bible, praying and asking God to set me free from this cycle. I would cry out in praise and worship. I needed a move that only God could provide.

I was desperate.

So much so that I took two weeks to limit my communication with other people. I didn't talk on the phone much and I stopped interacting on social media. I needed to be alone, just me and God.

My church had planned a 4-day revival the last week in June and I was preparing to get my breakthrough. I was determined that after this revival the chains would be broken. Not just off of my life but that eventually, the words my Pastor had spoken over me would come true and that alcoholism would no longer have power over my entire family. The generational curse would be broken.

Chapter 9
Finally Set Free

To say the least, the revival was powerful. The experience actually gave me the push I needed to finish writing this book and to finish telling this story; to finally put a period where I tried to put a comma.

I believe from the bottom of my heart that I have been set free. I would be a fool to turn back now! I have made up in my mind and heart that I would walk this earth alone before I pick up another alcoholic beverage. I am no longer afraid of what people will say or think and I am fully convinced that this is a forever thing. No more doubt.

This is the final chapter, there will be no turning back nor any added pages about how alcoholism made its way back into my life! I have been set free!!

Cycle Breaking Suggestions

You absolutely must be fully convinced before attempting to break a cycle or you will allow the devil room to get in and change your mind.

I am not saying you have to have it all figured out, but you do have to believe in your decision. For example, people asked me if I planned on not drinking ever again or just temporary. At the time I didn't believe that I could stop drinking for good. This gave the devil room to creep back in after time had passed. He knew I was unsure, so he used that doubt to get me back.

You need to determine your 'why'. Why do you want to break the cycle?

I read a book titled *Millionaire Success Habits* by Dean Graziosi. He wrote about how important it is to determine why you want to be successful. He explained how the reason needs to be a meaningful reason so that when you are faced with challenges you do not buckle.

For example, if you want to lose weight so you can have a flat stomach, that will not be a strong enough reason that will get you out of bed at 5 a.m. to go workout when you'd rather be sleep. But if you decided you want to lose weight so that you can live a long healthy life and be active in your kids and grandkids lives, that's going to carry you through the tough times.

You need a support system.

Another reason why I wasn't successful the first time is because I did not have a support system. It isn't anyone's fault but my own because I never asked anyone to be there for me when I was feeling weak. Anytime you are trying to break a cycle or do anything you've never done before, seek support. Having accountability partners or people who are on the same path as you, will help you when you feel weak.

You must stay in God's presence every day!

The temptation will come. If the devil tempted Jesus, he will most definitely tempt you. This is why it is important to stay in God's presence. It's important to always be praying, worshipping, attending church services, serving with other believers, fasting and reading the word. I used to think, "It don't take all of that." But it truly does take all of that!

You need to know God's truth (his word) for yourself.

I believe I was easily persuaded back into drinking because I did not know God's word for myself. The bible is filled with stories about the consequences of drinking. Too often we focus on Jesus turning water into wine and we miss everything else the Bible says about wine (alcohol).

Here are just a few scriptures. Again, I am not a bible scholar and by no means am I trying to throw scripture in your face. These are just some scriptures that can help when temptation tries to persuade you.

Wine and beer make people lose control; they get loud and stumble around. And that is foolish.
~Proverbs 20:1 (ERV)

Loving pleasure leads to poverty. Wine and luxury will never make you wealthy.
~Proverbs 21:17 (ERV)

Lemuel, it is not wise for kings to drink wine. It is not wise for rulers to want beer.
~ Proverbs 31:4 (ERV)

You should know that you yourself are God's temple. God's Spirit lives in you. If you destroy God's temple, God will destroy you, because God's temple is holy. You yourselves are God's temple.
~1 Corinthians 3:16-17 (ERV)

Don't be drunk with wine, which will ruin your life, but be filled with the Spirit.
~Ephesians 5:18 (ERV)

You should know that your body is a temple for the Holy Spirit that you received from God and lives in you. You don't own yourself. God paid a very high price to make you his. So honor God with your body.
~1 Corinthians 6: 19-20 (ERV)

In the same way, the men who are chosen to be special servants have the respect of others. They must not be men who say things they don't mean or who spend their time drinking too much. They must not be men who will do almost anything for money.
~1 Timothy 3:8 (ERV)

Understand that you do not have to be an addict to quit.

I remember being in school studying substance abuse. Every time someone would describe a substance abuser, I'd say to myself "That doesn't describe me, so I'm good." I had created an image in my mind of an alcoholic and because I did not fit that image, I did not believe I had a problem. But the truth is, problem or not, God was calling me to do something different and I needed to obey his call.

You don't have to feel like you have a problem to stop a cycle or bad habit. Maybe you just want change. Maybe you want to create a new family tradition. Breaking cycles and bad habits is all about becoming a better version of yourself.

You must be honest with yourself.

One thing I quickly learned is that if you want something to die you must stop feeding it. You have to be honest with yourself. If you are trying to stop doing something you may have to change your friend group, your hang out spot, your music, etc. For me, I know that sometimes I am triggered by seeing women drink wine on TV. By being honest with myself I know I cannot watch that type of stuff when I am feeling weak.

So anyone who thinks they are standing strong should be careful that they don't fall. The only temptations that you have are the same temptations that all people have. But you can trust God. He will not let you be emptied more than you can bear. But when you are tempted, God will also give you a way to escape that temptation. Then you will be able to endure it.
                      ~1 Corinthians 10:12-13 (ERV)

Lastly. Take time to heal without distractions.

Growing up in a home filled with domestic violence and alcoholism brought a lot of pain and feelings of abandonment. For years, I was searching for peace in relationships and drinking. I needed time to learn what actual peace felt like. Once, I began to experience peace regularly, I was finally able to start healing. Taking time to heal also helped me to discover my purpose and who I am. For years, I did not know who I was. I looked at my family and friends and tried to imitate what I saw. I did not know that I could be unique and different.

Thank you, Lord, for revealing to me that I am set apart, that I have a special place in your heart and that I am no longer a slave to my old self.

~Amen

Epilogue

Before I leave you, I want you to know that my mom is happily married and has been for six years. She finally found someone capable of treating her with the gentle love and kindness that she deserves. My stepdad is really good for her and a great addition to our family. Together they joke and laugh like two teenage kids. I believe it is through this newfound happiness that she has finally reached a place of peace and joy within herself.

Also, like I mentioned before, my mom is my best friend and I love her so much. She has literally been there for me through it all. Even when I was a wreck and would do stupid things like drive drunk, she never judged me. She's been by my side every step of the way on this new journey of becoming who God has called me to be. Even when she doesn't understand why I fast as much as I do or why I attend church as often as I do, she does her best to support me.

Truthfully its hard walking this path I've been called to walk and some days I ask myself why? Why do I strive to live a righteous life and why have I chosen to follow Christ? But then I remember my story. I thank God for my story because it made me who I am.

I could have written about so many other experiences that God saved me from. For example, I could have talked about the time I went bar hoping with some friends that lead to me spending the night in jail being charged with an assault and battery felony or the time I drove drunk for four hours from one part of Florida to a different part after using someone else's ID to go clubbing with some friends.

My goodness! God was truly covering me!

I thank God for covering me with his protection when I made those life-threatening decisions and I thank God for loving me when I didn't even know how to love myself. Through it all, I have been shaped to live a life filled with purpose, knowing who God is and who I am in him.

I pray that this book provides encouragement for anyone who is struggling with making a cycle breaking change in your life. With God, anything is possible. And I do mean anything. No matter how many times you fall, do not give up. Every day you wake up, is a new day to try again!

Made in the USA
Monee, IL
03 February 2021